YOU MUST REMEMBER THIS

1940

MILESTONES, MEMORIES, TRIVIA AND FACTS, NEWS EVENTS, PROMINENT PERSONALITIES & SPORTS HIGHLIGHTS OF THE YEAR

TO : *Zona*

FROM : *Mom.*

MESSAGE :

selected and researched
by
betsy dexter

WARNER  TREASURES™

PUBLISHED BY WARNER BOOKS

A TIME WARNER COMPANY

Warner Books, Inc.
1271 Avenue of the Americas
New York, New York 10020

Warner Treasures is a
trademark of Warner Books, Inc.

W A Time Warner Company

CAROL BOKUNIEWICZ DESIGN
PRINTED IN SINGAPORE
FIRST PRINTING : SEPTEMBER 1995
10 9 8 7 6 5 4 3 2 1
ISBN : 0-446-91072-4

'40

It was the year America began to prepare for war.

newsreel

Franklin Roosevelt, reelected in November, asked Congress for defense appropriations of $4.29 billion and production of 50,000 airplanes a year. Congress created the Selective Service System, the first U.S. peacetime program of compulsory military service. The new draft required all men between ages 21 and 36 to register.

In reply to Prime Minister

winston churchill's

appeal for aid, the U.S. sent surplus war supplies to England. President Roosevelt subsequently ordered an embargo on shipments of scrap iron and steel to all nations except Britain and those in the Western Hemisphere.

BY CONGRESSIONAL EDICT, THE 40-HOUR WORK WEEK WENT INTO EFFECT.

THE SMITH ACT

required the registration of all aliens and made it illegal to advocate the overthrow of the U.S. government by force.

IN SEPTEMBER, A GROUP OF ISOLATIONISTS FORMED **THE AMERICA FIRST COMMITTEE** TO PROTEST PRESIDENT ROOSEVELT'S FOREIGN POLICY AND TO KEEP THE U.S. OUT OF WWII. AMONG ITS PROMINENT MEMBERS WAS **CHARLES LINDBERGH. JOSEPH KENNEDY, SR.,** RESIGNED AS AMBASSADOR TO BRITAIN IN NOVEMBER, TO "HELP THE PRESIDENT KEEP THE UNITED STATES OUT OF THE WAR."

The U.S. census reported the population at 132 million. The average household was 3.8 persons. The median age was 28.9. Due to a historically low birthrate, the decade's gain was the smallest ever recorded. More than 56 percent of the population lived in places of 2,500 or more population. The life expectancy of a U.S. citizen was 63 years.

There were 264,000 divorces in the U.S.

Germany invaded France and entered Paris. The Vichy government of Occupied France, under Henri Philippe Pétain, signed an armistice with the Nazis.

headlines

international

In the North Atlantic,

german u-boats

began attacking Allied shipping. German submarines blockaded British ports. The British navy sank or captured the French fleet at the Battle of Oran to prevent it from falling into German hands.

IN EUROPE

German armies invaded Denmark, Norway, Holland, Belgium and Luxembourg. The Dutch and Belgian forces surrendered.

GERMANY BEGAN ITS BOMBING OF LONDON. GERMAN AND BRITISH PLANES BEGAN FIGHTING AIR BATTLES OVER BRITAIN. THE BRITISH RESPONDED WITH NIGHT BOMBING OF GERMANY.

The number of AXIS POWERS was expanded as Italy and Albania joined in.

In Tibet, a new five-year-old

dalai lama

was discovered and enthroned.

Italy declared war on Great Britain and France, attacking the British in North Africa and forcing the French to surrender. The British subsequently pushed back Italian troops in Egypt and invaded Libya.

In Pittsburgh, residents offered a $1 million reward for capture of Adolf Hitler alive and unhurt.

FOUR BOYS LOOKING FOR THEIR LOST DOG DISCOVERED A PREHISTORIC CAVE NEAR MONTIGNAC, FRANCE. **THE GROTTE DE LASCAUX** FEATURED A MAIN CAVERN AND SEVERAL GALLERIES, ALL DECORATED WITH ENGRAVED AND PAINTED ANIMALS.

STILL IN ITS INFANCY, THE NEW MEDIUM OF TELEVISION BROADCAST THE REPUBLICAN NATIONAL CONVENTION FROM PHILADELPHIA.

In painting, **MAX ERNST** completed *EUROPE AFTER THE RAIN,* a work known for its "calm violence." **PAUL KLEE**'s *DEATH AND FIRE* foreshadowed his own cremation later in the year.

Laurence Olivier and Vivien Leigh

Raymond Massey and **Ruth Gordon** starred in John Cromwell's movie ***Abe Lincoln in Illinois*** at the New York Music Hall. The Metropolitan Opera presented ***Othello.*** **Laurence Olivier** and **Vivien Leigh** opened in ***Romeo and Juliet.*** **Joan Fontaine** appeared in Hitchcock's ***Rebecca,*** based on Daphne du Maurier's novel.

cultural
milestones

shopping spree

MAN'S UTILITY ROBE, **$7.50.**
WOMAN'S CASHMERE PULLOVER SWEATER, **$8.95.**
NORWEGIAN BLUE FOX JACKET, **$165.**
PACK OF MARLBOROS, **20¢.**
ENGLISH CORK DARTBOARD, **$2.97.**
THREE DARTS, **29¢.**
ONE-PIECE WOOL BATHING SUIT, **$29.95.**
FIELD GLASSES, **$14.00.**
MAN'S RAYON "LOUNGING ROBE," **$15.00.**
WOMAN'S RAINCOAT, **$7.95.**

THE MUSEUM OF MODERN ART ESTABLISHED ITS FIRST SEPARATE DEPARTMENT OF PHOTOGRAPHY.

newspaper editors' of america top radio stars of 1940

Champion of Champions — **Jack Benny**
Outstanding New Star — **Dinah Shore**
Comedian — **Bob Hope**
Comedienne — **Fannie Brice**
Comedy Team — **Fibber McGee & Molly**
Comedy Series — **"The Aldrich Family"**
Male Vocalist — **Bing Crosby**
Female Vocalist — **Kate Smith**
Dramatic Show — **"Lux Radio Theater"**
Dramatic Series — **"One Man's Family"**
Daytime Serial — **"Vic & Sade"**
Quiz Show — **"Information, Please"**

Crime and comedy dominated the airwaves. Most popular underworld dramas were **"The Shadow"** and **"Gangbusters."** Favorite yuck-fests were **"Fibber McGee & Molly"** and **"The Jack Benny Show."**

radio

Commercial radio celebrated its 20th birthday.

8

On March 23, NBC radio premiered

"truth or consequences,"

a spoof of giveaway quiz shows. Ralph Edwards became radio's #1 gamesman as the host of this slick show. Contestants who failed to answer simple quiz questions had to "suffer the consequences" and participate in some outlandish, usually slapstick, punishment.

The networks covered the election of President Roosevelt with vigor. Political parties paid high prices for air time, recognizing the vote-getting power of radio.

THE FCC ruled that companies could operate FM radio and television stations on a commercial basis. Start-up dates for these services were January 1 for FM and July 1 for TV of the following year. The war limited the start of both these media due to a shortage of materials needed for production of sets and transmitters.

science

Professors at Oglethorpe University, in Georgia, deposited a bottle of beer, a movie fan magazine, an encyclopedia and thousands of other objects in their **"CRYPT OF CIVILIZATION,"** a time capsule to be opened in the year 8113.

JAMES HILLER AND V. VLADIMIR ZWORYKIN FURTHERED THE DEVELOPMENT OF THE ELECTRON MICROSCOPE.

AUSTRALIAN OPHTHALMOLO- GIST N. M. GREGG DISCOVERED THAT GERMAN MEASLES CON- TRACTED DURING PREGNANCY MAY CAUSE BIRTH DEFECTS.

Engineer Peter Goldmark developed the first commercially practical system for broadcasting color TV.

DEATHS

Philip Nowlan,
creator of the Buck Rogers comic strip, died of a stroke in Philadelphia on February 1. He was 52.

Luisa Tetrazzini,
celebrated Italian diva, died on April 28 at 68.

Marcus Garvey,
black nationalist, died on May 10.

Paul Klee,
visionary abstract artist, 61, died of a heart attack in Muralto, Switzerland.

Walter Chrysler,
the auto tycoon who founded the company that bore his name, died on August 18.

births

JACK NICKLAUS, golf pro, aka The Golden Bear, January 21.

SMOKEY ROBINSON, singer, February 19 in Detroit, MI.

MARIO ANDRETTI, race car driver, February 28.

HERBIE HANCOCK, jazz keyboardist, April 12 in Chicago.

AL PACINO, actor, April 25 in New York City.

RINGO STARR, ex-Beatle drummer, July 7 in Liverpool, England.

PELÉ, soccer star, born Edson Arantes do Nascimento on October 23 in Brazil.

RAQUEL WELCH, actress and fitness video hostess, September 5 in Chicago.

RICHARD PRYOR, comedian, December 1 in Peoria, IL.

milestones

Leon Trotsky
died on August 21 in Mexico City.

Sir Joseph John Thomson,
winner of the 1906 Nobel Prize in physics for experiments in conduction of electricity through gases, died on August 30 at 83.

F. Scott Fitzgerald,
the novelist who chronicled America's Jazz Age, died of alcoholism on December 21.

F. Scott Fitzgerald

variety's top 15 sheet music tunes of 1940

1. south of the border
2. oh, johnny
3. scatterbrain
4. careless
5. indian summer
6. in an old dutch garden

'40 hit music

7. when you wish upon a star
8. woodpecker song
9. playmates
10. make believe island
11. god bless america
12. i'll never smile again
13. blueberry hill
14. ferryboat serenade
15. only forever

MILLION-SELLING RECORDS

San Antonio Rose (Decca) — Bing Crosby

In a Shanty in Old Shanty Town (Decca) — Johnny Long & His Orchestra

Pennsylvania 6-5000 (Decca) — Glenn Miller & His Orchestra

Frenesi (Victor) — Artie Shaw and His Orchestra

San Antonio Rose (Okeh) Bob Wills & His Texas Playboys

ON A PATRIOTIC NOTE, IRVING BERLIN CONTRIBUTED ALL ROYALTIES FROM "GOD BLESS AMERICA" TO THE BOY AND GIRL SCOUTS OF AMERICA.

Jazz pianist, composer, and orchestra leader Duke Ellington reached huge popularity this year.

THE EXODUS OF EUROPEAN COMPOSERS BROUGHT THE U.S. A WEALTH OF WORLD-CLASS TALENT. **ARNOLD SCHOENBERG, BÉLA BARTÓK,** AND **IGOR STRAVINSKY** ALL FLED NAZI PERSECUTION TO LIVE AND WORK IN AMERICA.

A LATIN DANCE CRAZE SWEPT THE COUNTRY THIS YEAR.

America was rhumba-crazy. Latin clubs sprang up everywhere, with club owners hiring rhumba bands to complement their U.S. orchestras. Arthur Murray capitalized on the Latin dance fad. Wedding the American Virginia reel with the Latin conga, he created the **"Americonga."** With swing bands all the rage among younger listeners, **the jitterbug** continued to thrive, and the Lindy Hop enjoyed renewed popularity. Saturday was "jitterbugging" night!

dancing

13

bestselling

14

Dylan Thomas published his short-story collection, *Portrait of the Artist as a Young Dog.*

books

T H E   P U L I T Z E R

John Steinbeck won the Pulitzer Prize for Literature for ***The Grapes of Wrath.***

William Saroyan won the Pulitzer in Drama for ***The Time of Your Life.***

Mark Van Doren won the Pulitzer Prize for his ***Collected Poems.***

A quartet of classic novels were published this year: Graham Greene's *The Power and the Glory,* Richard Wright's *Native Son,* Carson McCullers's *The Heart Is a Lonely Hunter,* and Raymond Chandler's *Farewell, My Lovely.*

IN BOXING

Joe Louis remained King of the Ring. On March 29, the reigning champion scored a second-round KO over contender Johnny Paycheck at Madison Square Garden. Two months later, on June 20, he again defended his title, flooring Arturo Dodoy in the 8th. This brought the Champ's record to 47-1, with 39 knock-outs. His total earnings rang in at $1,704,341.

the 12th summer olympics,

scheduled for Japan and then Helsinki, Finland, were canceled on account of war. The Winter Games, slated for Japan and then the town of Garmisch-Partenkirchen, in Germany, were also scrapped, due to a clause in the Olympic Charter which states that the games cannot be held in any country that is "an aggressor at war."

THE CHICAGO BEARS WERE NAMED THE CHAMPIONS
IN THE PRO FOOTBALL PLAYOFFS.

IN AUTO RACING,
DRIVER **WILBUR
SHAW** WON THE
INDY 500 FOR THE
SECOND YEAR IN
A ROW.

sports

**The New York Rangers defeated
Toronto, 4 games to 2, to snag
hockey's Stanley Cup.**

In college football, 19,200 fans
turned out on New Year's Day
to see Southern California beat
Tennessee, 14–0, in the Rose
Bowl. Navy also blanked Army
14–0, in their annual matchup.

**In baseball, the Cincinnati Reds
squeaked past the Detroit
Tigers, 4 games to 3, to win
the World Series. The National
League won
the All-Star
game with
a 4-0 shutout.**

17

oscar winners

Best Picture **Rebecca,** Selznick/UA, produced by David O. Selznick

Best Actor **Jimmy Stewart, The Philadelphia Story**

Best Actress **Ginger Rogers, Kitty Foyle**

Best Supporting Actor **Walter Brennan, The Westerner**

Best Supporting Actress **Jane Darwell, The Grapes of Wrath**

Best Original Screenplay **The Great McGinty,** by Preston Sturges

Best Adapted Screenplay **The Philadelphia Story,** by Donald Ogden Stewart

Appearing this year in *Seven Sinners*, blonde temptress

marlene dietrich

was asked by the Nazi government to return to her native Germany and make pictures there. Dietrich reportedly replied, "No, thank you."

clark gable

made film history, signing a contract with Metro for $2.1 million — the largest sum ever paid a movie star.

MAE WEST AND **W. C. FIELDS** MADE THEIR FIRST JOINT APPEARANCE THIS YEAR IN *MY LITTLE CHICKADEE.*

top ten box-office actors

1. Mickey Rooney

2. Spencer Tracy

3. Clark Gable

4. Gene Autry

5. Tyrone Power

6. James Cagney

7. Bing Crosby

8. Wallace Beery

9. Bette Davis

10. Judy Garland

It was a busy year for pretty-boy actor **RONALD REAGAN.** On March 14, Warner Brothers announced that Ron was the right man for the role of Notre Dame's George Gipp in *Knute Rockne — All American.* Post-"Gipper," Reagan starred with Rosemary Lane in the not-quite-classic *She Couldn't Say No.*

movies

Charlie Chaplin's *THE GREAT DICTATOR* was released in October. Critics dubbed it "as disturbing as it is hilarious." Chaplin played a dual role as a Jewish barber and "Der Phooey, Adolf Hynkel." The barber was modeled after Charlie's much-beloved friendly tramp. "Der Phooey" was a madman who batted around a beach-ball globe of the world.

hit movies

1. *Pinocchio* (Walt Disney Productions) — $32,957,000
2. *Fantasia* (Walt Disney Productions) — $28,660,000
3. *Boom Town* (MGM) — $4,586,000
4. *Rebecca* (Selznick/United Artists) — $1,500,000
5. *Santa Fe Trail* (Warner Brothers) — $1,500,000

PINOCCHIO WAS WALT DISNEY'S FOLLOW-UP TO THE SMASH HIT *SNOW WHITE AND THE SEVEN DWARFS.* IT WAS GIVEN THE UNHEARD-OF BUDGET OF $2,600,000 — ABOUT $50,000,000 IN NINETIES DOLLARS.

This year's Automobile Manufacturers' Association show featured a wider range of colors than ever before. Colors were made more lustrous by use of metallic pigments. Two-

cars

The big trend in new cars was wider seats, longer bodies, more glass area and stiffer construction. tones were displayed at many exhibits. The most popular body style was the 4-door, 6-passenger sedan, followed by the 2-door sedan.

POWER-OPERATED WINDOWS WERE THE HEIGHT OF LUXURY.

DIRECTION SIGNALS WERE MADE AVAILABLE ON MORE MODELS THAN EVER.

the jeep, developed by U.S. Army Quartermaster Corps and built by Willys, made its debut this year. Its name came from the sound of the first letters of its job description: "general purpose." The newfangled vehicle was capable of operating on rough terrain, thanks to its high clearance and 4-wheel drive. The Jeep offered a great variety of military uses: command car, or ammunition and personnel carrier.

'40

The war put an end to feminine frippery.

To be chic was to be suitably dressed for the occasion: easy-fitting, light-colored town suits replaced dark, wasp-waisted clothes. Due to

fashion

In October, Pope Paul denounced women for "bowing to the tyranny of fashion." Nobody mentioned his hat.

fabric shortages, last year's bouffant skirts were rejected in favor of a much slimmer silhouette. Hips were the focal point of the spring collections, with swathed polonaise skirts, the fullness gently gathered and released at the back and the bodice extended to a point.

final factoid

the first nylon stockings were sold in the united states.

archive photos: inside front cover, pages 1, 2, 5, 6, 8, 10, 11, 13, 14, 15, 21, 23, 25, inside back cover.

associated press: pages 2, 3, 4, 6, 16, 17.

photofest: pages 7, 9, 13, 18, 19.

photo research:
alice albert

coordination:
rustyn birch

design:
carol bokuniewicz design
mutsumi hyuga

'40